Atlas of Urban Mythologies

Atlas of Urban Mythologies

Francesca Cocchiara and Sergios Strigklogiannis

to Natalia

Crane in Klybeck — Kleinbasel; Basel, Switzerland (June 2022)

On Myths, Cities,

and Other Monsters

Imagination is what makes us humans.

Entire new worlds can exist in our minds, and storytelling is what connects us to one another. Every story travels, from those narrating it to those who receive it and later pass it on in their own way. Stories cross boundaries and the lives of many, changing how we see ourselves, others, and what surrounds us, as long as they can always be rewritten, re-appropriated, and re-narrated. Otherwise, they lose their magic, and they are dead.

Another great power that comes with narratives, and particularly with myths, as they describe specific contexts, is that one can actually find reality beyond the layers of imagination. The fantastic manipulation staged in fictional stories gives body to actual matters that are otherwise easily overlooked. Quoting Roland Barthes: 'However paradoxical it may seem, myth hides nothing: its function is to distort, not to make disappear'.[1] For this reason, we decided to explore myths in the real land of cities, quintessentially fascinating and complicated places where mythology manipulates reality to raise awareness of otherwise invisible issues.

There is a tendency to associate myths with past cultural beliefs and stories without actual connection to reality. So, we started from here and asked ourselves: what can contemporary myths add to present-day cities?

What we discovered is that urban environments are filled with living mythologies. Some are visible on the skin of buildings, some emerge in the ways people describe their surroundings and give names to them – just like characters in a story –, and some date back to ancient times and formed the city's cultural image. In other cases, some stories are still waiting to be told.

For us, mythology is a medium for communication: open, accessible, and malleable. And, like all good stories, it is real. Of course, we don't mean literally real – it's pretty unlikely that one can speak with a Big Yellow Duck or a Pyramid. Nevertheless, in this *Atlas*, myths give voice to the voiceless, uncovering the untold urban stories of gentrification, division, the threats of urban commons, spatial injustice, and what you might wish to add to it.

Here we bring you this collection of urban mythologies. We hope they make you want to embark on a journey and find our characters in their real settings, just like our narrators did.

Urban Mythologies are a common ground:
You can appropriate them.
Urban Mythologies are malleable and transformable:
You can rewrite them.
Urban Mythologies are a way of asking questions:
It's okay if you don't have answers – yet.

Map of the Journey

Oslo
Copenhagen
Dublin
Berlin
Eindhoven
Prague
Danube
Rhine
Vienna
Paris
Basel
Graz
Ljubljana
Zagreb
Sarajev
Arles
Ligurian Sea
Adriatic Sea
Barcelona
Rome
Madrid
Balearic Sea
Tyrrhenian Sea
Lisbon
Sea of Sardinia
Cagliari
Ionia
Alboran Sea
Sea of Sicily
Mediterran
Libyan

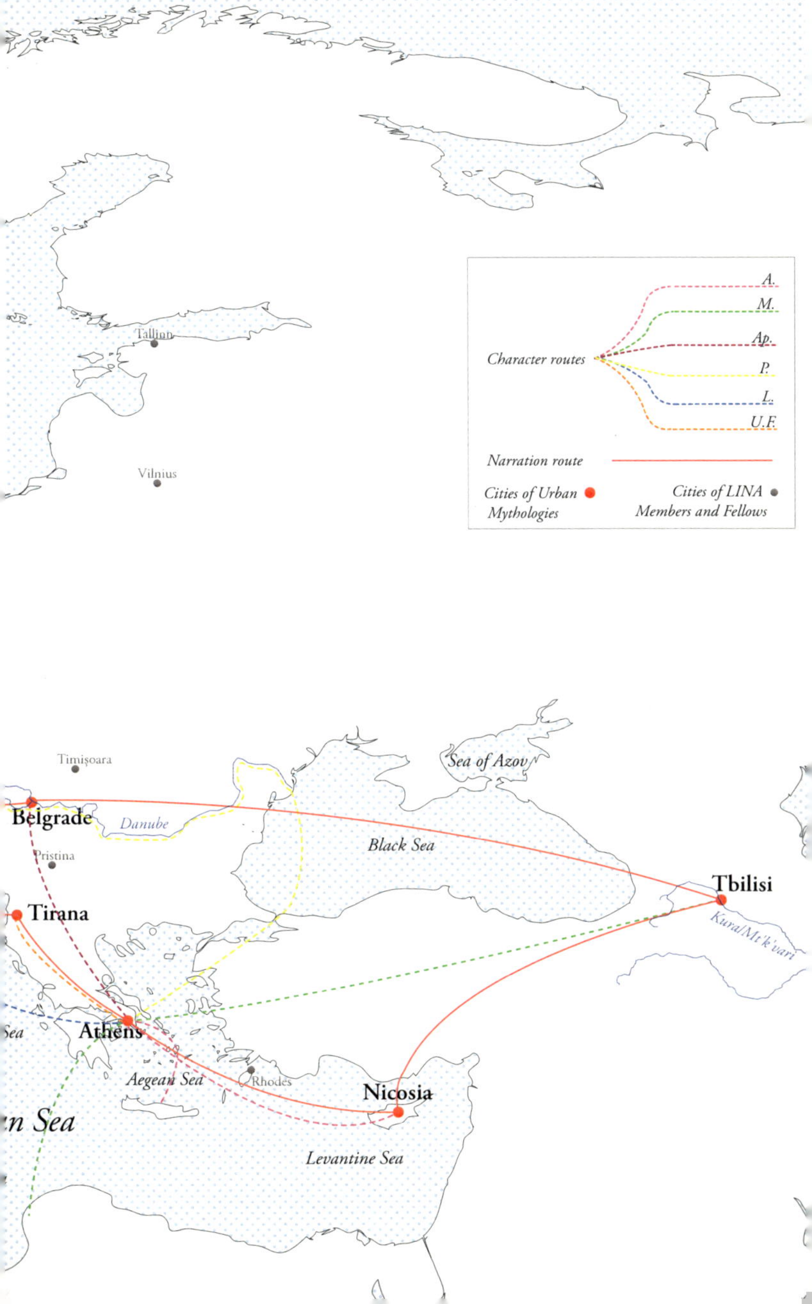
A.
M.
Ap.
P.
L.
U.F.
Character routes
Narration route
Cities of Urban Mythologies
Cities of LINA Members and Fellows
Tallinn
Vilnius
Timişoara
Sea of Azov
Belgrade
Danube
Black Sea
Pristina
Tbilisi
Tirana
Kura/Mt'k'vari
Sea
Athens
Aegean Sea
Rhodes
Nicosia
n Sea
Levantine Sea

Chapters

1 Looking for Khôra

Athens, Greece

"As you set out for Ithaka
hope your road is a long one,
full of adventure, full of discovery.

'Apocalypse Now', mural by INO (2020);
Athens, Greece (December 2021)

It is about to begin.

We are all here, waiting for the protest to start, and it's great to have you with us on this journey.

We met at the usual place in front of the Academy, and everyone arrived on time or even earlier. Once more, we are many, maybe five or six thousand, and people are still arriving.

Although first, let us introduce ourselves: there are six of us to accompany you on this adventure. Sorry that we can't introduce ourselves by name – you know, we can't quite trust you yet, and perhaps names aren't even needed. You should know that each of us had a mythical past, but luckily, nobody really cares in this crowd.

Indeed, we prefer to stay anonymous for now because people – probably also you – tend to believe the myths written about us and not by us. Those where they lied; they changed the facts, where they gave us the role of those who committed the original sin, the ones who were defeated, the ones who were lost. They called us witches, demons, or strange creatures; they even called us monsters, or in some cases, we just silently helped someone else become a hero. Yet nevertheless, one thing is certain, we were never lost nor defeated; we were never evil nor dead, as they would say – no, no, no. Oh! Forgive me. I digress and forgot to tell you how on earth all six of us found ourselves together here in this city and at this demonstration today.

A. came one night from her island to Athens by boat, and she wandered lost for some time in the city until she found the thread of her life again. *P.* always dressed in black, used to live in a nearby city before moving to our neighbourhood. She would disappear every now and then – she never told us why, and we never asked. *U.F.* is a ubiquitous figure. You would meet them everywhere in the city, in any neighbourhood, as if they could be in many places at once. They would be everywhere you can imagine, waiting, with their long neck, black wavy hair, and half-closed eyes, as if dreaming and crying at the very same time. *L.* is a dog-like nomad creature living every day in a different neighbourhood. Always showing up in times of struggle, you can always count on him, there at the forefront. *Ap.* is the big enigma. We have never seen their face, but their gaze passes right through you and makes you wonder what they are up to.

Now it's my turn. Oh, you must know me... In their myths, they called me a monster, cursed, stone blind. They wanted my head, especially the Goddess of this city, because – you know – a monster is repulsive when alive, but everybody wants a piece of it when dead. And yet, here I am. No, we didn't know each other before, but as soon as we met, we realised we were all connected by common fears and a shared sense of otherness, so we became family for one another.

We all live here in this district close to the city centre: however, we know it won't last long. After the crisis, 'Operation New Athens' started and changed everything: the people, the neighbourhoods, the rents, and our everyday lives. They are trying to take us – and people like us – out of our houses because more and more visitors from distant countries want to see this mythical city; or because more 'important' people than us want to live in the heart of the city. For them, we were always the freaks, the monsters, the queers, the unwanted, the invisible, the dangerous 'other', just because we never matched the image of the city. They simply bring more money with them, and since we were never welcome to begin with, we will be the first to go.

For a long time, this neighbourhood was the only place in the city where we weren't afraid, where creatures like us could be themselves. Now, this is changing fast. The square, our parks, police on every street… they came to clean, purify, and sterilise our city, neighbourhood, streets, houses, bodies, and minds. They want to wipe out delinquent creatures like us, and this made us furious. So, here we are at the protest. Only here can we be ourselves, here we feel safe, here nobody judges the way we look, our past, our choices.

The blocks are now raising their banners, and some of the first slogans are heard, a sign that we will soon start our path through the city. At this very moment – before the first step – all of us always have a feeling of mixed excitement, agitation, and anxiety. I think the Germans call it *Reisefieber*.

{Movement}
And here we go!
We start moving like two dancers: us and the guards of New Athens. Everything in the city will feel different from now until we return home.

{Stop}
We stop in front of a closed jewellery shop. As always, *Ap.* was there, waiting for us to join the march. As soon as they saw us, they donned their balaclava and walked into the crowd to meet the rest of us.

{Movement}
We are swarming the city streets, and every step is part of a spontaneous choreography. More of us are joining; we can see their heads from afar: The Seed People of

Navarinou Park. They hold a banner that reads:
'You did everything you could to bury me, but forgot that I am a seed'.[2]

{Stop}
We arrive at the square and turn towards the Parliament. More guards of New Athens are lined outside, and we are sure that something will soon disrupt our movement, rhythm, and delinquent dance.

So, better we leave you with some final words. As you are about to discover in the following chapters, we have been on a long search for a place where we – the invisible, the forgotten, the queers – can express ourselves, a place for being, the Khôra.

We explored alone different cities across the continent, as we didn't know each other back then. We captured our journeys in this Atlas you are about to read: they were lonely explorations in *terrae incognitae,* and yet they served us to understand where our Khôra is.

We part ways now. Take the Atlas, and we will meet again soon.

{An explosion goes off}

'Seed', mural by Blu (2017); Navarinou Park in Athens, Greece (December 2022)

'Loukanikos', mural by Billy Gee, Alex Martinez, N_Grams (2014); Psirri in Athens, Greece (December 2022)

2 Caged Birds Sing
Nicosia, Cyprus

‘Untitled’ by Sonke; Psirri in Athens, Greece (January 2023)

Writing in front of the Kunstmuseum Basel;
Basel, Switzerland (June 2022)

Acknowledgments

Laistrygonians, Cyclops,
angry Poseidon – don't be afraid of them:
you'll never find things like that on your way
as long as you keep your thoughts raised high,
as long as a rare excitement
stirs your spirit and your body.

Watchtower on the Green Line; Nicosia,
Cyprus (October 2022)

What an unbearable sound!

Where is it coming from? I hope it stops soon – I can't stand it anymore! It has been drumming in my ear since I arrived in this city. Sometimes, it sounds like a hum or buzzing, and the next moment like a dissonant song or instrument; but whatever the sound, it is always insufferable!

It could be the wind that blends noises from everywhere in the city. Or perhaps I got travel sick, and it's just a sound in my head. Indeed, it wasn't a good idea to travel by boat to this island. The trip took thirty hours until we reached the port of Limassol, and from there, I needed another two hours by bus to arrive at my destination. Yes, the wind and the seasickness must have affected my hearing.

So many hours have passed, and I can still hear it. I walked around the medieval city walls, forming a perfect circle, and I observed that it was louder and more annoying when I was closer to that dividing buffer zone. But it can't come from there, the place is sealed with barricades and has been abandoned for many decades. Inside this no man's land, what is left is ruins. Only through the checkpoints can one pass from one side to the other, and even then, one is not allowed to stop there. As far as I know, no human nor creature can enter.

But that sound, that sound... there it is again.

My best explanation is that it comes from a bizarre military vehicle or machine. There are so many of them around. What a strange city. There are all kinds of borders here: stone walls, constructions blocking the way, barricades made with concrete-filled oil drums, medieval fortifications, wooden fences, wire meshes, new metal barriers with watchtowers, informal street blocks constructed with old signs, boom barriers with sentry boxes on the side, and of course, checkpoints. I read somewhere that the only things that move at checkpoints are winds, spirits, and eyeballs – and in this city, I understood that it's true.

I'm about to give up any hope of discovering where the murmurs I've been hearing all day are coming from. I don't know exactly where I am, but I can tell I am outside the walled city, as I can see the walls on my right. I have to cross to the other side of town, and I know there is an entrance somewhere around here.

I take out my passport to pass the checkpoint for the hundredth time today. A man in uniform checks it and gives me a stern look as he returns it to me. It's already dusk, and the sun, almost hidden behind the medieval walls, creates peculiar shadows on the street. I always thought there should be a different word for dusk or night shadows other than those of the day.

I'm halfway between the two checkpoints, and on my left side I see an old hotel with an Asian-looking façade. It's getting dark and I can't quite read the sign... PALACE something. Who cares? Oh, there it is again! But this time, the sound is less annoying than before. In fact, it reminds me of the noises of an outdoor market accompanied by a rhythmic drum beat. I must find out where it's coming from. I check in both directions to see if any guards are looking towards me before leaving the asphalt street into the so-called Green Line. I'm walking in-between the two walls, and now the sounds are not only louder but different again. Is it a piece of music, just voices, birds chirping or flying up above? I have to get closer.

I realise I'm not alone.

I see some shadows on the stone wall. I immediately take

out my camera. I'm not allowed to take photos here – I know from the countless warning signs – but I can't resist, and I take three consecutive shots. I follow the shadows, and the previous desert landscape has given way to a completely different setting. Wild vegetation, palms, orchards of orange and lemon trees, olive trees, and many other plants had reclaimed this residual space while creeping ivy and bougainvillaea have taken over the surrounding walls, making their stones almost invisible. Here and there, I can see constructions that look like houses made of wood or small shops. I'm still trying to overcome my surprise as I follow the shadows walking along a lush jungle-like path.

And here it is!

There's a clearing at the end of the path in this small forest. A crowd has gathered, drinking, laughing, and chatting loudly among one another. All kinds of creatures, humans, and spirits from both sides of the divided city, are having fun together. At one point, I even spot the siren Leucosia speaking with her grandmother Mnemosyne. Apparently, it's some kind of festival or celebration because a punk rock band is playing music, and everyone I meet is either drunk or on their way. The front-person of the band is a siren singing magically. I have no idea why the melodies and the cheerful sound of laughing seemed so awful before, when I was walking along the borderlines.

I order a beer from a small wooden kiosk. I try to pay but as I figure out, my money is useless here. It seems that these liminal creatures have their own rules and have established their state hidden between the walls, in this leftover space, this buffer zone, the Green Line. This is a city beyond Nicosia, home to the marginal, the forgotten, the ones that wanted to forget, and the invisible.

I finished my beer, and I'm leaving now. On my way back, I remember the siren Leucosia and a verse from a poem by Maya Angelou comes to my mind:

The caged bird sings
with a fearful trill
of things unknown
but longed for still
and his tune is heard
on the distant hill
for the caged bird
sings of freedom.

Green Line at night;
Nicosia, Cyprus (October 2022)

Abandoned UN Watchtower in the Green Line;
Nicosia, Cyprus (October 2022)

Barricades in Nicosia's old town;
Nicosia, Cyprus (October 2022)

Abandoned UN Checkpoint.
Nicosia, Cyprus (October 2022)

3 No God's (Is)land
Tbilisi, Georgia

Laistrygonians, Cyclops,
wild Poseidon – you won't encounter them
unless you bring them along inside your soul,
unless your soul sets them up in front of you.

Views of the Mt'k'vari River's Magic Garden;
site visit for the Tbilisi Architecture Biennial, a project
by the Center of Contemporary Art (CCA).
Photo courtesy of Studio Inscape (April 2023)

The trip through Turkey was long and full of surprises, and I thought I wouldn't make it on time for our meeting as I lost the last ship yesterday night. Fortunately, there are many ferry routes daily – almost every half an hour.

There hasn't always been an island in this city. It appeared, or better to say, it was created some years ago, and this is one of the most important matters I would like to discuss with the locals. I already contacted some people and invited them to come, but I mainly wanted to speak to Her. She is known by many names – Adgilis Deda, Mother of Locality, Place-Mother – and for being the protector of places, the spirit of each *topos*. What I didn't know and read about recently is that she also takes care of travellers – of everyone who travels with the body or mind, of everyone in motion or standing still in the places she protects. Therefore, as part of my personal search, she is the most well-suited person to talk to, and perhaps give me hope that I can find it.

Our appointment was on Monday at four o'clock in one of the old city's cafes. I found them all sitting at a round table, and I think I must have interrupted a quarrel because they stopped yelling as soon as they saw me coming.

The table was full of empty glasses of chacha (ჭაჭა) and ashtrays full of cigarettes. I sat between Adigilis Deda (ადგილის დედა) and a Kura loach, fish that showed clear signs of heavy smoking. Around the table also sat Mt'k'vari River (aka Kuna), the deity Tskarishdida (წყარიშდიდა), and a liquid person.

After some formal introductions with the guests and ordering a new round of drinks, I got straight to the point as we didn't have much time. I switched on my voice recorder and put it on the table.

{Me} Just so you're all aware, I've started recording now. When did it happen? When did they come up with the idea?

{Adgilis Deda} They started some years ago. I don't remember precisely when.

{Mt'k'vari River} I do remember exactly the day. It was a shock for me, a shock I never recovered from... They've reshaped me and my tributaries many times over the past centuries, but I could never have imagined they would do something like that.

The times before, I could somehow understand it. Throughout my entire length – from the Caucasus to the Caspian Sea – there was always a need for drinkable water, irrigation for agriculture, and energy. Even if this made my water turbid and polluted, I kept finding excuses since it was for their survival. But this? This is... it's insane!

{Adgilis Deda} You are right. I found myself in a difficult position here and didn't know what to do. How could I be the protective spirit of this place and the people that travel in it? This is why I quit. Now I am the spirit of nowhere and the protector of nobody, let alone the tourists arriving to enjoy the fake island and its artificial beaches.

{Me} And how did they manage it? I mean, how did they plan and come to construct all this?

{Mt'k'vari River} The initial idea was to separate a portion of the city by redirecting part of my body via small canals. They said it be good for the image of the city, for the economy, for its residents, and so on and so forth. In the beginning, they said it would be only for three months – June, July, August – and for the rest of the year they would shut the canals, and my body would return to its previous shape. Nevertheless, as the flow of tourists increased, they extended it for the whole year. At that point, there were still bridges connecting my two sides. Then they decided to take more, transforming my banks, and tearing me apart – and here it is, an island!

{Liquid person} Yes, this is how it happened, but it's not only that. I used to live in one of the neighbourhoods that later became part of the island. Soon after all this had started, our neighbourhood became a resort, our houses hotel rooms, and our everyday became stories in social media. Eventually the rents were prohibitive, and I had to leave the island and adapt to a new life.

{Adgilis Deda} And who knows what's next...

{Tskarishdida Goddess} Who would have guessed it? An island in the South Caucasus. And you know what? Before creating the island, they considered building an archipelago inside the city's reservoir – or sea, as they call it – as they did somewhere in the Black Sea.

{Smoking Fish} They never asked our opinion, though. We demanded many times for a referendum, and we even sent an official complaint to the Parliament and a letter to the United Nations, but finally, they 'democratically' decided themselves... And you? What have you done? Supposedly, you were on our side, keeping us and our waters safe.

{Tskarishdida Goddess} There was nothing I could do. The same as in the Tbilisi sea, and all dams, canals, all the changes to the Mt'k'vari's current. How about the situation in your city? Hey, somebody order another round, please?

{Me} Kifissos, Iridanos, Ilissos, all of them were rivers crossing the city, but now they have been buried under the city, and roads have been built over them – only cars flow across them now.

{Smoking Fish} Cheers! What were we saying? Ah, yes... Some scientists warned that this could not last long. But as we know, there is nothing more permanent than the temporary. Uff, my drink and my tobacco need a refill.

{Me} Is this why everyone is demonstrating now in the city's mainland?

{Adgilis Deda} Also for this... But wait, is there a demonstration on now? Why did nobody tell me? I'm sorry, I have to leave right now.

As soon as Adgilis Deda left, I switched off the recorder. The others were too drunk to be of any help. I called the waiter over for the bill.

Views of the Mt'k'vari River's Magic Garden; site visit for the Tbilisi Architecture Biennial, a project by the Center of Contemporary Art (CCA). Photo courtesy of Studio Inscape (April 2023)

Dighomi Meadows upstream of the Mt'k'vari River; site visit for the Tbilisi Architecture Biennial. Photo courtesy of Studio Inscape (April 2023)

4 The 45th Destruction
Belgrade, Serbia

Hope your road is a long one.
May there be many summer mornings when,
with what pleasure, what joy,
you enter harbours you're seeing for the first time;

La Santa de Beograd, mural by Remed & The Arts (2008);
Belgrade, Serbia (February 2023)

By the river, here's where I found them.

I was still on my boat, passing under the bridge, but I decided to drop anchor there at the Sava amphitheatre once I saw them. They were immersed in conversation, so I went unnoticed and pulled out my camera.

One of them must have been a deity, her adorned hair and dress looked like those from ancient times, but her face was ageless. She sat on her throne the whole time, showing signs tiredness and resignation more than once. By her side stood a giant holding a tree in its hand. I was expecting it would smash it with its concrete jaws wide open, but somehow it didn't. In front of the giant, an army of six sergeants settled down; they were all proudly coated in red suits, showing their side profiles, and speaking in sync. Next to them sat a massive, wet, inflated yellow duck. It didn't seem bothered by the large banner stuck under its belly, and I wondered what was written on it.

I hit record. Here is what I heard them saying:

{Vinča Goddess} I smell it. It's the dust in the air and everything that goes wasted. It's going to happen again. A black wave is slowly overtaking one neighbourhood after another, and before we know it, the whole city.

{Tree Eater} Now you smell it? I've been screaming about this for years to literally every person coming and leaving the town, but nobody seemed to listen.

{Six Sergeants} Perhaps your mouth is large, but your voice is weak! We would have...

{Tree Eater} What have you done? Couldn't at least one of you see when waves of troopers came to destroy my neighbourhood at night?

{Six Sergeants} By then it was already too late!

{Big Yellow Duck} It's never too late. We stormed the streets soon after and tried to stop it *en masse*, with all our powers. So many humans came with us! In some marches, we were thousands and...

{Tree Eater} As much as I'd have liked it to, your protest didn't bring my neighbourhood back. They tore it down, masked like ghosts. Savamala *tabula rasa*. Go there now and see the few buildings you can find, abandoned, and emptied. If you're lucky, you'll see some graffiti. Some colours on the ruins, at least.

{Vinča Goddess} It was a cursed night, I recall. But the Tree Eater is right, everything was already poisoned long before that. It started when the decision was made to build it here, and now it's expanding throughout the city like a black wave. Time is ticking. It's happening again. The 45th destruction of the city will be completed. And I have witnessed all of them...

{Big Yellow Duck} Nothing is over yet! People are alert now. We won't let it happen on our watch.

{Six Sergeants} Then look at the reflections on the water. There it is! Greed buys everything, and this city is no exception.

{Big Yellow Duck} Before we give up, I say let's ask for Her help. La Santa is the only one that might have a solution.

{Tree Eater} Her, you say? She is helpless. I can see it well from here.

{Six Sergeants} For once, we agree with you. We don't expect anything from Her.

{Vinča Goddess} We shall try. I'd like to have a little hope.

Then, the duck carefully unfolded the wrinkled banner and pulled it up under its neck, looking straight ahead as if to show it to somebody. I could finally read it and thought it was a plea: 'Don't Let Us D(r)own'.

The last figure to join the group came at this very moment. Embracing a mesmerising chaos with her long wings and vest, and yet a sense of peace shined through her presence. They all turned to look at her and listen to what she had to say:

{La Santa de Beograd} I carry contradictions, growth, mistakes, prosperity, bad and good intentions, destruction, and creation. I retain the memory of all identities that took form in space and time, and I let them be. All this coexists in my body, and through my body, is unified. I protect the meanings attached to the rhythms of life, represent all of them, and keep them all together. What I cannot preserve is what does not belong to me. I abandon what is disguised as spectacular, but is nothing other than an imposition. I reject the façades behind which are no souls. For all this, I am no shelter, no place to call home.

All the creatures are left silent, looking towards the glass tower at Sava's waterfront. My camera's battery starts blinking red.

Mural and billboards in Savamala;
Belgrade, Serbia (February 2023)

Tree Eater, mural by Blu (2009);
Belgrade, Serbia (February 2023)

View of the Belgrade Waterfront Project and the Kula Belgrade skyscraper; Belgrade, Serbia (February 2023)

Urban ruins in Savamala neighbourhood;
Belgrade, Serbia (February 2023)

5 Hybris
Ljubljana, Slovenia

may you stop at Phoenician trading stations
to buy fine things,
mother of pearl and coral, amber and ebony,
sensual perfume of every kind–
as many sensual perfumes as you can;
and may you visit many Egyptian cities
to learn and go on learning from their scholars.

Jason killed it. He and his comrades founded this city and sealed it with arrogance. Are we all humans born with the egotism to believe we can tame nature to our liking? They slew the protector of this land, and this was the hybris.

From the Black Sea into the Danube and then through the Sava until the Ljubljanica River, this is how I got here. As I passed through the last city, I could tell it was doomed. It's a transitional place crossed by two forces: one comes from the mountain and one from the sea. These two forces used to be balanced in their coexistence, but we exacerbated their power, and the city is left with no patron to mediate these extreme conditions.

In front of me, a vast expanse of meadows, swamps, and channels that I'm about to explore as I try to remediate the first act of violence that happened here a long time ago. I hope to find another protector for this city, a living being that is willing to restore the dialogue between its inhabitants and nature.

I don't have much time before the flood comes. Off I go.

I wasn't expecting to find this kind of dwelling – since I've always seen them pictured over bodies of water – but here it is, above the marshy ground: a palafitte. The piles are driven into the soft, peaty soil and hold up a wooden platform on top of which stands the hut. The thatched roof overhangs the timber-framed walls, covered with reeds to their full height except where two tiny windows open, one per side. Indeed, such a pile dwelling fits perfectly into this landscape as the tall stilts would keep whoever was living there safe from flooding.

I would definitely not have thought of seeing someone living there nowadays, but to my surprise, I see a man bustling around. He's replacing one of the piles of his house – well, it must be his house, I suppose. Our gazes cross and he interrupts what he's doing, so I come closer, but he anticipates me and talks first.

'Why are you here?'

'I didn't mean to seem intrusive. I'm here to seek help.'

He scans me from head to toe, frowning.

'You seem to be just fine. Who needs help? Forget it. I'm not helping anybody anyways. I came here to stay away from the city and from problems. I already have my own.'

'Ljubljana is fevering. I'm looking for a creature – or a person, why not? – willing to keep the city safe and show people how to live in harmony with nature again.'

Meanwhile, the palafitte man sits down, resumes his work on the pile, and starts milling its tip.

'And why do you care? Do you live there?'

'No, I'm just a visitor. I'm on a long solo journey, but I know who the first traitor of these places was. I wish to write another story for this city, one in which it can prosper.'

Now, he stands up and looks at me, straight into my eyes.

'I fled Ljubljana thirty years ago, at the early signs, and I came here to coexist peacefully with the landscape. You must make space for the flooding. You must not fight it. This is what my palafitte teaches me every day. There's no way I'm going back to the city now, let alone to look after it. Let it be cursed how it is; I can't do anything about it.'

Then he turns his back and withdraws inside. As I walk away, I hear him saying one last word.

'Go by the fields and ask some creature there, if you care so much. They're used to living by the farmers, and maybe they're willing to help you.'

In a veil of mist, I take one of the myriads of paths that crisscross the marsh. I hear the sound of nature, the sum of

Views of the Ljubljana Marsh (*Ljubljansko barje*).
Photo courtesy of Vesna Petkovska / Slovenian Ministry of Natural Resources and Spatial Planning

all the voices of those who inhabit this place. The rustle of leaves in the wind, the patter of birds on the surface of the water, the humming of insects, the croaking of frogs. I stop by a mosaic of wet meadows and fields hedged by alder trees and a network of watercourses.

I have mixed feelings about what I see. The picturesque beauty of this landscape is overwhelming but somehow, I realise that it must have been altered in ways I cannot perceive. I come closer to one of the alder trees and stand underneath its shadow, looking at the short-stalked, oval leaves. Wet grass grows at its base, and birds chirp from the upper branches. I touch its trunk.

'You are protecting these fields, I can tell.'

The voice of the alder tree is serene.

'We belong here. We're rooted in water, and there's nowhere else we would like to be. So, in exchange, when winds are strong, we offer shelter to the wildlife.'

'I know it seems very far away, but the city is at threat. Even the abundance of green spaces can't help. Would any of you wish to become the guardian of an inhospitable land and, with your wisdom, help it endure this situation?' A gust of wind passes through the leaves as if the tree were sighing.

'Humans burned it, the organic soil where I sink my roots. It had taken several thousand years to form and was depleted in just over a century. So, you see, certain mistakes are irreversible. Perhaps the city just needs to accept that.' I point at the fields. 'Is it already too late? Is a flooding of no return coming soon?'

I never get an answer, but I return to my boat and go up the Ljubljanica river heading back to the city, puzzled, with a question in my mind and heart. The way we humans have modified these wetlands throughout history is by listening increasingly less to the rhythm of nature and being more in control of it. Or at least thinking we are.

Is the nemesis inevitable for crimes committed against nature?

Views of the Ljubljana Marsh (*Ljubljansko barje*).
Photo courtesy of Vesna Petkovska / Slovenian Ministry
of Natural Resources and Spatial Planning

6 Flâneuses

Basel, Switzerland

Keep Ithaka always in your mind.
Arriving there is what you're destined for.

Helvetia auf der Reise, sculpture by Bettina Eichin (1980).
Basel, Switzerland (June 2022)

The train station (page 16)
We finally arrived.

I put a bookmark in my travel guide to avoid losing my page and got off. The trip was long and complicated, but who cares. Now I'm here, and I've heard so much about this city before. The people we came with disappeared quickly after the train stopped. Understandable since we're all in such a hurry nowadays.

I had to be creative on my way here because it's challenging to enter this country without a passport – actually, every country on this continent. I didn't plan to stay for long, just for some hours, and I had to be at the port to board the ship in the afternoon. So, I walked down to the city centre where – according to my travel guide – all the museums, galleries, and art exhibitions the city is famous for are located.

Gross Basel (pages 24–55)
I wandered through the narrow streets of the old town from the Museum of Fine Arts and strolled around the commercial district. I found myself in front of a red building with a tower. The city precisely matched the pictures of my travel guide. It's so tidy and clean. I saw some people in uniform accompanying a woman with colourful clothes and a headscarf. Maybe they didn't like her music or how she dressed, or perhaps they were worried she didn't match the images in my travel guide. I noticed a guy in a suit who was taking his basilisk for a walk and asked him for directions, as I needed to cross the river. He gave me a strange look, stuck his tongue out at me – for a reason I never understood – and pointed to a bridge without saying a word.

The Lällekönig on the Mittlere Brücke;
Basel, Switzerland (June 2022)

Mittlere Brücke (pages 56–64)
I started crossing the bridge. The first thing I noticed was a memorial dedicated to all witches – actually, to the ones that didn't survive their rage. Unfortunately, the inscription was in German, but there was a translation in my book:

Basel commemorates the people accused of witchcraft, persecuted, tortured, and killed in earlier centuries. Today this place reminds us to meet other people without prejudice and not to exclude them.

I looked under the bridge and saw from afar people swimming in the river holding something like a balloon – what a strange way to commute. I noticed three figures almost drawn in the water near the bridge's foundations. I couldn't see them well, but one must have been an enormous bird, the other looked like a giant cat, and the third seemed to be an old man. They were completely still, like statues.

Walking towards the other side, I saw someone sitting on a wall at the edge of the bridge. A woman with her back turned to the street, gazing towards the industrial area at the city's borders, with her bare feet dangling over the river. Yet, with her big suitcase, she also had the appearance of a nomad or a wanderer like me. I asked her for directions, as an excuse to speak to her, curious to know who she was. She didn't even look at me or turn her head. Finally, after a while, she stood up and signed me to walk together.

I was surprised to see her leave behind her heavy shield with the cross, her spear, and some of her clothes. I made the motion to bring them to her, but she waved me not to. She probably didn't need them anymore.

Kleinbasel (pages 64–70)
So, we entered Kleinbasel together. I checked my travel guide to find out that this district has significantly less information and photos of places to visit. The buildings, the streets, the sounds, the shops, the people, and even the looks are different in this neighbourhood. A man approached us and asked us something in a language I didn't understand. My companion took out two francs and gave them to him. I noticed that the coins had a hole in the middle. We turned onto a street named Klybeckstrasse to arrive at Dreirosenbrücke; from there, the port was nearer.

Klybeck (page 71–half page)
We walked down the street to reach the neighbourhood of Klybeck, and there I thought to check my city guide to get some information, thinking that maybe there was an art gallery or exhibition somewhere close to visit. Surprisingly, only half a page of my city guide was dedicated to Klybeck, and the photo was blurred. Strange.

Next to us, I noticed a woman walking down the street within a zone marked with a dashed green line. She stopped abruptly at the end of this zone, exactly where a green line was. She looked like she wanted to continue walking down the street with us, but something like an invisible wall blocked her way.

The remaining pages of my city guide are unreadable, so I decided to tear out the page with the map and leave my travel guide with this woman. She might need it one day if she decides to visit the city on the other side of the river, because, for this part, there is nothing.

We lost sight of her as we turned towards the river.

Streetwalker space;
Basel, Switzerland (June 2022)

Only the map (page 80)
We headed towards a crane lit by the sunset. From afar, its metal silhouette looked like a giant dog. We passed under it and entered the railway buffer area between the river and Klybeck. We continued walking silently along the abandoned tracks, leaving the still train cars behind us. The more we walk, the more it feels like we are always at the same exact point. Only stubborn wild greenery broke the monotony of this repetitive pattern between the two parallel steel rails, the wooden slabs, and the stones. I stopped to check my map to discover that this whole part of the city didn't really exist there.

At the port (without a city guide or map)
We are now at the port. I'm standing in front of the ship, and she is just behind me. I was sure she would board with me, but to my surprise, she left. As I found out later, she rented a small apartment in Klybeck, and works in a small neighbourhood cafe.

Crane in Klybeck – Kleinbasel;
Basel, Switzerland (June 2022)

Terrain vague, Klybeck;
Basel, Switzerland (June 2022)

7 Kaleidoscope
Tirana, Albania

But don't hurry the journey at all.
Better if it lasts for years,
so you're old by the time you reach the island,
wealthy with all you've gained on the way,
not expecting Ithaka to make you rich.

Tirana's Pyramid; Tirana, Albania (2019).
Photo courtesy of Saimir Kristo

As I stepped inside, I was warned by a solemn voice: 'In just a blink of an eye, everything here changes.' I wanted to see it for myself, so I asked the Pyramid: 'Can you show me? If I look through your glazed walls, would I be able to catch at least a fragment of this city?' Surprisingly, the concrete monolith laughed in response. 'Oh, this city is a mosaic of countless pieces, the question is not if you can get to see a few, but how will you make sense of all of them. How you'll avoid getting dizzy!' So, I leaned towards the sloping glazing. The Pyramid was my kaleidoscope, and the city an ever-changing pattern. I looked.

...

A wide-open heart. It must be the heart because it's right at the centre. People can walk across this vast space on any path they want. The sun, the rain, and the wind find no obstruction, this square and the sky are in direct dialogue. From here you see the past, the present, and the future, the impossible skyline of this city.

Broad asphalt avenues, stone-paved streets, a mosque, high-rise towers, palazzi, an orthodox church, monumental façades, far away mountains, symmetry, haphazardness, domes, boxes, pillars, stacks, blue, white, yellow, red, green, untouched grass, a statue, a bell tower, flags, cranes... And something missing.

...

Something is missing. There's a sudden void in the urban fabric. On the ground there are traces of collapse and the footprints of fights. Vegetation springs up as a *memento mori*: we – people and our artifacts – all go back to the earth. But this one must have been a violent loss. I can tell because nobody is rebuilding, no construction site, everywhere is full of cranes but here. Perhaps they're still mourning about it. It must have been recent.

I step back but can't take my eyes off the window. 'What was there?', I ask. 'If you look for the meaning of what is there and what is not, good luck with that.' 'Then, what changed is lost forever? What about the memory of it?' 'There's no time for memory here. We have to keep up with the new course of things. We've been standing still for too long', closes the Pyramid." So, I change the view.

...

Car anarchy. Streets are so packed with cars, trucks, buses, and motorbikes that the smog of their engines thickens into clouds of fog. I can't hear it, but my mind automatically recalls the loud cacophony of car horns and I become agitated. It's chaos. With my eyes I follow a car pulling over and occupying the pedestrian crossing. No hope they can find parking. The driver turns the hazard lights on and quickly gets out of the car. He hurries to the other side, opens the rear door, and helps his child get out. Hand in hand, they briskly walk on the sidewalk, slaloming in front of cars, scooters, lamp posts, holes, and scaffolding until they arrive at the gates of a school. After dropping off his child, the man runs back to his car to find out that somebody has parked their truck behind him. He gets mad and opens the door to honk relentlessly until another angry man comes to move it away. Both of them carry their frustration into their cars and will breathe it for the next few hours while queuing at the traffic lights. Is it better to breathe anger or smog? I blink and the view changes.

...

5-star certificate of excellence. A blue-coated glass roof zigzags above brimming market stalls. The space looks lively and colourful. A couple in shorts and sunglasses with two large backpacks grab some burger patties and thank the vendor.

Despite everything seeming new – the paint on the surrounding buildings is still vibrant – I feel this must be an old neighbourhood because that's where grand bazaars are normally found. So, I look closely to see traces of some past. I glimpse the top of a minaret. I move my sight further.

Cars again. Medium- and low-rise concrete buildings with street-front shops. Construction sites. Suddenly a stone footbridge, but I see no water underneath. Inside my kaleidoscope, I look south.

...

Another wide square, sided by light-coloured monumental buildings. I linger on their symmetry and rational order until a shiny tower catches my attention. It's red, but it also reflects the sky. It raises from the podium of a nearby building. Oh, I get it now, it's the landmark of an arena. On a closer look though, I see this is not the only skyscraper near the venue. Then I wonder and ask the Pyramid, 'Do these towers serve to guard the place?' 'Let's say they ... offer what is needed to bring a contemporary spirit to the city.' For a moment I think how exclusive it must be on the top floor and watch the game from above.

...

The Pyramid was right. I'm overwhelmed by this multitude of things. I think I've seen enough, but something still piques my curiosity. 'What about this place? What's your story?', I attempt to ask. 'Well, I'm not that old if this is what you are wondering. But I survived. My bones are made of solid concrete and this – like it or not – lives a long life, so I have plans for my future too... unless they tear me down at some point. I don't exclude it.'

Then I collect my things, I look up at the point where all the concrete beams radiate and take a deep breath. 'I hope you stay where you are and that you can reveal the city again, to many.' This was my heartfelt wish to the Pyramid, my kaleidoscope over the dazzling Tirana.

Time to hit the road again.

Skanderbeg Square (*Sheshi Skënderbej*);
Tirana, Albania (2019). Photo courtesy of Saimir Kristo

8 Finding Khôra

Athens, Greece

Ithaka gave you the marvellous journey.
Without her you wouldn't have set out.
She has nothing left to give you now.
And if you find her poor, Ithaka won't have fooled you.
Wise as you will have become, so full of experience,
you'll have understood by then what these Ithakas mean."

'Ithaka', by C.P. Cavafy.[3]

{Following the explosion}

We marched. We screamed. We inhaled tear gas, and we ran until we ran out of breath. But today, we defended the only thing left to us, our right to be.

We're heading back towards our neighbourhood. It feels like time expanded, but it's been only a few hours. Without the need to arrange it, we knew we would meet at the park close to where the Homeless Giant sleeps. Today we saw him, though. He joined the protest, of course he did!

We sit on the benches to rest – our feet are on fire! – and we find each other to see if everyone is safe. We are glad to see that you made it here too, after travelling through our *Atlas of Urban Mythologies*. Are you trying to find out where each of us went? Truth is, the cities and their own myths are more important than us individually. And if you are asking yourself whether we found Khôra after all these journeys, we can tell you: Khôra doesn't exist.

Yet it happens.

It appears ephemerally for shorter or longer periods, and when it does, a third, magic space is created, a city beyond the city, one that overcomes the physical and mental borders that divide us emerges.

Khôra showed up beneath our soles as we marched the streets. Khôra was where all of us – mythical creatures, humans, giants, rivers, speaking animals, legendary places, pyramids, and other monsters – became visible again, had a voice and could be ourselves regardless of our otherness.

So, Khôra happens together, in common.

They are coming for us again.

'No Land for the Poor', mural by Wild Drawing (2015);
Athens, Greece (March 2023)

Revealed

Realities

From 2008 to 2018, Greece went through a period of economic austerity that resulted in the impoverishment of a large part of its population. In response to the harsh crisis, the government rebranded the image of the city by prioritising the tourism industry over the needs of its less affluent inhabitants and effectively turning the struggle of their daily survival invisible.

With this market logic in mind, public spaces have been redefined as commodities for the visitor-customer-consumer, excluding alternative uses, restricting accessibility, and expelling non-conforming social groups. Moreover, the explosion of short-term rentals paved the way for a gentrification that is sharpening housing issues and homogenising the use of urban space by mining the rich diversification that Athens used to host: informal meetings, demonstrations, street vendors, micro-economies, daily survival practices, or any other alternative use of space.

Housing auctions and evictions increase the number of homeless and those living in precarious housing conditions, which combines tragically with the arrival of victims of the refugee crisis and results in an expanding, vulnerable social group of urban nomads excluded from the right to the city.

The Green Line is a demilitarised buffer zone patrolled by the United Nations Peacekeeping Forces that extends approximately 180 kilometres through the Cypriot state and divides the capital in two. Since 1974 the north of the island is claimed and militarily occupied by Turkey and the city of Nicosia lies right in the middle of this de facto division between Greek and Turkish Cypriots. Along the Green Line, watchtowers and checkpoints overlook the guarded crossings between the two sides, after an almost thirty-year no-crossing ban.

The Green Line does not have a uniform appearance. In some parts of the old town, it shrinks down to a few metres wide, while in other parts of the island it stretches to a few kilometres, incorporating small, inhabited villages.

In its run through the city of Nicosia, the Green Line is often described as a dead zone for being largely untouched, abandoned and out of time, contained by concrete walls, metal gates, barbed wires, and barrel barricades. Nevertheless, within this thick border, flora and fauna are gradually taking over, thriving in the near absence of hunters and most other human interference.

Lying on the banks of the Kura River, the city of Tbilisi has historically been deeply connected with the element of water. During the times of the Soviet Union, an artificial reservoir known as the Tbilisi Sea was built in the northeast of the city for irrigation purposes, and later in 1985, hydroelectric power generation on the Kura river secured Tbilisi's supply of electricity as well as water.

The Kura is considered one of the most stressed river basins in Asia because of its extensive transformations to accommodate irrigation, municipal water supply, and hydroelectricity generation. On one hand, the creation of water reservoirs in the Kura, and also in the merging river of Aragvi at the north of Tbilisi, is appealing for tourist and recreation industries. Yet, on the other, it poses at least the question of how sustainable this man-made landscape alteration is. In fact, due to the dam operation in these artificial bodies of water, when they release the water – to match the peak needs from the capital city –, flooding of entire territories occurs, submerging the natural and cultural heritage of the nearby territories for several months until the water dries up.

The urban fabric of Belgrade reflects multiple layers of growth: the European-looking historical centre; the expansion of the new Belgrade during the socialist era; the chaotic extension of the city to the east; the culture-led transformation of neighbourhoods such as Savamala. The balance of all Belgrade's co-existing identities is being disrupted by the Belgrade Waterfront Project, which is paving the way for mega-projects as drivers of the future city's development.

Planned by the Serbian Government in cooperation with partners from the United Arab Emirates, the BWP arises in the prime location of the Sava amphitheatre, one of the city's most valuable visual and recreational areas. Its construction started in 2014 and by its completion, it will include high-end residential units, luxury hotels, offices, and malls, targeting upper-class inhabitants and foreign investments. The way the BWP was planned and implemented is a perfect example of neoliberal urban development and the epitome of aggressive top-down urbanism. Massive demonstrations were organised in 2016 when the majority of the Savamala neighbourhood was demolished overnight to give space for the BWP, turning what until then was a vibrant neighbourhood into urban ruins.

Ljubljana

Albeit modest in size and with plenty of green spaces, the Slovenian capital is warming up fast. Some surveys have it as the world's fastest-warming city, with an expected average annual temperature rise of +3.5 °C by 2050. The city is situated in a valley with low airflow and at the meeting point between two climate zones particularly affected by global warming: the Alpine region and the northern Mediterranean. It is self-evident that Ljubljana alone cannot change its destiny without a proper European climate policy. Extreme weather conditions are likely to happen, affecting both the city and the rich landscape of its wetlands.

The Ljubljana Marsh (Ljubljansko barje) is Slovenia's largest complex of wet grasslands, well-known for its rich biodiversity, which results from specific cultivation practices. Most of the land is privately owned and safeguarded as part of a natural reserve. Home to prehistoric settlements of pile dwellers, the marshland has been radically man-changed by draining the area for farming, construction, and domestic heating purposes. The highly organic soil was discovered to be a fast burner, and heavy peat extraction took place in the 19th century, considerably reducing the marshes' surface level and subsequently its capacity to drain water.

Basel

The city of Basel is historically, administratively, and geographically divided into two parts, Grossbasel and Kleinbasel, with the latter being considered a working-class and immigrant district. However, everyday life in Kleinbasel – particularly in certain neighbourhoods such as Klybeck – creates spatialities and imaginaries that seem to break Basel's dominant image and narrative as an art and cultural capital or as one of the most liveable cities.

In this colourful, multicultural, and less privileged part of the city, poverty, socio-spatial injustice, and alternative imaginaries coexist with the threat of gentrification. Over the last few years, the demand for housing in Klybeck boosted, on the one hand, due to the attractive character of the neighbourhood and, on the other, because of top-down projects for the urban regeneration of the Klybeck area. All this resulted in a sudden and overwhelming increase in rental prices and is about to radically change its character.

Tirana

The recent history of Tirana is characterised by a series of occupations and regained freedom that is visible in its multifaceted urban fabric. After gaining independence from the Ottomans, the city endured the fascist occupation. Its liberation however, turned into a new communist regime that isolated the Albanian capital until 1992. From then on, population growth, car ownership, and unruly building took off and resulted in the chaotic urban development that continues today at a fast pace to meet the goal of achieving Tirana's next makeover.

Given the country's weak economy, the promises of modernisation rendered via cutting-edge architecture, lush greenery, and car-free mobility are, in practice, quite controversial. Private-public partnerships lacking transparency and considerable real estate investments with unknown funders are pushing gentrification and jeopardising the city's building heritage with no proper regulation.

Glossary

of Mythical

Characters

Adigilis Deda
ადგილის დედა
A deity in Georgian mythology representing the protective spirit of the place (*genius loci*), often referred to as 'the mother of locality' or 'place-mother'. She was worshipped as the patroness of both the locations and the visitors travelling there.

Alder tree
A genus of trees, planted in lines at the edge of wetland plots and widely found in the Ljubljana Marsh, capable of absorbing excess water from the ground.

Ariadne (A.)
A Cretan princess in Greek mythology who was known for helping Theseus to find his way through the labyrinth, with the help of her red thread, and kill the Minotaur. After being abandoned by him on the island of Naxos, she is found by Dionysus who marries her.

Apocalypse Now (Ap.)
Mural created by artist INO in 2020 in the Athenian neighbourhood of Psiri representing a person with a full-face balaclava looking as if they are just about to move into action. The title cites the famous war film by Francis Ford Coppola, and plays on the ancient Greek meaning of the word 'apocalypse', which is 'uncovering' or 'revelation'.

Big Yellow Duck
Symbol of the grassroots movement 'Do Not Let Belgrade D(r)own' (*Ne Davimo Beograd*) formed in 2014 in opposition to the Belgrade Waterfront Project. The big

inflatable duck was always present in the demonstrations across the city and in the river Sava.

Helvetia auf der Reise
Sculpture created by Bettina Eichin in 1980, located in Basel's Middle Bridge (Mittlere Brücke). It depicts a woman sitting on a wall, looking across the Rhine, and leaving her belongings behind her. The artist reinterprets the Helvetia allegory shown on the franc coins by representing a woman who frees herself of the burdens of her life and embarks on a journey.

Homeless Giant
Reference to the mural by artist WD in 2015 entitled 'No land for the Poor', in the neighbourhood of Exarcheia in Athens. The artwork depicts a sleeping homeless person on the façade of a building and is dedicated to 'the poor and homeless here and around the globe'.

Jason
Legendary Greek founder of Ljubljana, along with his companions the Argonauts. After stealing the Golden Fleece from King Aetes, he travelled across the Black Sea up to the Danube, Sava, and Ljubjanica waterways, and there in the marshlands, he killed a dragon that would later become the symbol of the city.

Khôra
The notion of Khôra dates back to Plato's text *Timaeus*. It has been discussed in philosophy, particularly by Jacques Derrida, to indicate a space-time with characteristics of otherness, where one can establish a sense of belonging, a place for being.

Kura loach (Smoking Fish)
Oxynoemacheilus brandtii
Freshwater fish endemic in the drainage basins of the Kura River in the Caucasus area. Its population is heavily affected by the creation of dams for hydroelectric power and pollution, resulting in its inclusion on the list of threatened species.

La Santa de Beograd
Mural created by the French artist Remed in 2008, located on Karadjordjeva Street and visible from Branko's bridge, the city's entrance. It is said that Belgrade has been destroyed and rebuilt around forty times throughout its long history, and this inspired the artist who wanted to symbolise a patroness for the city.

Leucosia
Λευκωσία
Name of the capital of Cyprus, in English known as Nicosia. In Greek mythology, she was one of the Sirens – half-human half-bird creatures with alluring voices – the daughter of the river-god Achelous and the muse Melpomene.

Liquid person
Reference to Zygmunt Bauman's concept of 'liquid life', a view on contemporaneity where precarity and uncertainty are endured through constant, necessary adaptation.

Loukanikos (L.)
Athens' riot dog that front-lined street protests in the capital during the crisis of the 2010s. Time Magazine listed it as one of the personalities of the year in 2011 for being a fearless protester.

Medusa (M.)
In Greek mythology, she was one of the three Gorgons – female-like winged monsters – and the only mortal among them. She was raped by Poseidon in the temple of Athina, who then punished her with the curse of serpent hair. Anyone who meet eyes with Medusa would turn into stone, and the demigod Perseus was sent to cut her head off. He slayed her, and used her head several times to defeat enemies, and then gave it to Athina who placed it in the centre of her shield to terrify her adversaries.

Mnemosyne
In Greek mythology she was the goddess of memory and mother of the nine Muses.

Mt'k'vari River
Mostly known as Kura river, it originates in the Greater Caucasus mountains, crosses the countries of Turkey, Georgia, Armenia, and Azerbaijan, and flows into the Caspian Sea.

Palafitte man
Reference to the prehistoric inhabitants of the Ljubljana Marsh. These pile dwellers were the area's first known farmers and metal workers from around 5000 to 500 BCE, settling across Europe on the edges of lakes, rivers, and wetlands.

Persephone (P.)
Daughter of Zeus and Demetra, she was abducted by her uncle Hades who took her to the underworld. She

would come back and forth to the surface, symbolising the cycles of vegetation. Persephone and her mother are the protagonists of the Eleusinian Mysteries, rituals representing the eternity of life.

Pyramid of Tirana

Structure built in 1988 as a museum dedicated to the Communist leader Enver Hoxha. With the collapse of the regime in 1991, the space became a conference centre and was used as a temporary NATO base in 1999. Example of brutalist architecture, the pyramid is now being renovated to become an IT centre for the youth.

Seed People

Reference to the mural in Athens by artist Blu in 2017 on a building facing Navarinou Park, a former carpark reclaimed and self-organised as urban allotments and a greenspace. The artist represents the community living in the neighbourhood as seeds that sprout, break the asphalt, and become dandelions spread by the wind to the rest of the city.

Six Sergeants

Šest kaplara

Residential towers built in the 1960s during the New Belgrade expansion belonging to the urban subdivision Block 21. They are referred to as the six corporals, as most apartments were home to military personnel and their families.

Tree Eater

Mural painted by the Italian artist Blu in 2009, close to Branko's bridge, between Savamala and the city centre. It depicts a giant face with a wide-open mouth and building-like teeth, eating a tree. The intent was to raise awareness of urban ecology issues resulting from the city's development.

Tskarishdida Goddess
წყარიშდიდა
Mermaid-like goddess of Georgian mythology, protector of rivers, lakes, and fishes.

Urban Fairy (U.F.)
Fictional name given to the unnamed artwork of Greek street artist Sonke widely found across Athens city centre. Shown in different variations, it depicts a person – most often a woman but not exclusively – with black, wavy hair, and closed melancholic eyes, often carrying messages of socio-political critique.

Vinča Goddess
Female deity worshiped by the Vinča culture and represented in the terracotta figurine, 'The Goddess on the Throne'. The civilization occupied a wide region of the Balkans around 5700–4500 BCE, and one of its archaeological sites is in a suburb of Belgrade, constituting part of Serbia's cultural heritage.

Vogel Gryff, Wild Maa, and Leu
Heraldic figures of Kleinbasel that are part of the local folklore and often recalled in the performances that stage the rivalry between the districts of Klein and Gross Basel. The sculpture of artist Ludwig Stocker entitled 'Lagerstätte', by one of the Middle Bridge's piers, depicts these three mythological creatures as floating on the surface of the water.

Featured

Fellows

As we said in the introduction, the *Atlas of Urban Mythologies* is a common ground. Throughout our narratives, we have indirectly disseminated eight mentions of innovative ideas developed by LINA Fellows within the Architectural Program 2022–2023. The authors presented their projects at the LINA Conference held in October 2022 at the Faculty of Architecture of Ljubljana. Due to their connection to the cities and the themes that constitute our Atlas, we have chosen to feature them in our stories. We wish to give resonance to their work so that they can inspire your reading further.

In the Athens chapters, our characters take part in a protest described as a choreography, a way to experience the city's space through the movement of their bodies. This is where we connect with Mirto Delimichali and her project *dwindledscapes_practices of affection*. A choreographer and researcher based in Athens, her work focuses on how our bodies experience space and connect with the landscape. Kinetic narratives emerge when we share our memories and feelings related to a place. Her project aims to find practices of affection and co-existence with the landscape, listening to its stories, past, and possible future through our senses.

In the chapter in Nicosia, the urban space reflects the past collective trauma of the city's division. Contested areas and borders resulted from the creation of a demilitarised zone separating the north from the south part of the city. How to inhabit these no man's lands is a question at the centre of Tevi Allan Mensah's work with his project *borderlands**. Architect and visual artist based in France, he explores the border as a complex territory and questions the role of architecture in shaping these spaces. As part of his research, he has envisioned a project for the Green Line of Nicosia, reopening part of it and transforming it into a series of pocket parks. This micro-environment between architecture and wilderness defends the hypothesis of an architecture without a program, without construction, to reconsider an immense territory through a simpler perspective.

The dialogue we staged in the Tbilisi chapter saw humans and non-humans interacting on a subject impacting their lives. Decision-making processes in cities are highly anthropocentric and overlook humans' deep connections with multispecies environments. Studio Inscape, with their project *Gestures of Care – Thinking through Networks*, developed a tool that promotes ecological thinking for an inclusive and integral design. Trained as architects and urbanists and with a strong orientation towards ecological philosophy, Charlotte von Meijenveldt, Willie Vogel, and Eileen Stornebrink created a workshop where they bring human and non-human actors together and let them talk about the future of their landscape in relation to pressing climatical challenges. As part of the Tbilisi Architecture Biennale, they applied their network thinking to the theme of bodies of water and the politics surrounding their use.

'Understanding City Growth' is the theme of the 2023 Belgrade International Architecture Week (BINA). As part of our residency with this institution, in the chapter dedicated to this city, we fictionally discussed an actual project that is considerably reshaping the development of Belgrade. Our narrator uses the medium of videomaking to capture the moment where a dialogue among mythical creatures, each representing an identity of the city, is happening. Fellow Rebeka Bratož Gornik was also involved by BINA to reflect on the changing building scene of the city, and she does so by using video documentaries as a methodological tool to explore architecture, social issues, and anthropology. As a freelancer researcher, she developed the project *Re-Function*, a documentary series presenting modernist buildings and ways for the public to make new use of them.

The underlying issue presented in the chapter of Ljubljana is urban warming. On this matter, we were informed by the work of Prostorož and their project *Hotspots – a bottom-up approach to urban heat*. The group is a non-profit urban design studio composed of an interdisciplinary team of architects, social scientists, and technical staff working on how to mitigate urban heat in the Slovenian capital. Starting with a simple but crucial question to the regular users of public spaces, on which part of the city gets too hot, they collected consistent data, gathered suggestions for initiatives for cooling measures, and identified specific hotspot clusters. Possible design solutions encompass diverse greenery, water-permeable areas, better maintenance, user involvement, more comfort for pedestrians and cyclists, attractive public transportation, and reducing car mobility.

In the Basel chapter, the city is walked through by two characters that face the changing of the urbanscape, its controversies, and occasionally its corners of in-between zones. These *terrain vagues* are common to many cities and explored in Swiss artist Jonathan Steiger's work. His focus lies at the intersection of landscape, aesthetics, and urbanism, and his project *Roadside Greenery* is a short film about the ephemeral landscape that stubbornly emerges at the sides of a motorway ring construction site. The S AM Swiss Architecture Museum of Basel involved him in a discussion on the topic of how unspectacular scenery and situations of the everyday can inspire a new form of aesthetics and ethics in architecture.

One of the recurring views that the narrator experiences through her kaleidoscopic view over the city of Tirana is car chaos. Traffic congestion is an urgent issue in the Albanian capital, and in our fictional narrative, we mention the difficulty of making space for slow living rhythms when it comes to school commuting, for example. As part of the Film Festival 'Leave No One Behind', co-organised by Barleti University, Atelier Filter Café Filtré developed a design solution around the notion of school streets in Tirana. The group started out from a citizens' movement and has extensive, hands-on experience organising open street events and advocating for low-traffic neighbourhoods. Their initiative *Openstreets22* is centred on the idea that through ad-hoc debates and imagining new ways of reappropriating streets spaces, concrete solutions can be implemented, leading to better air quality, traffic safety, and increased liveability in cities.

At the beginning of the Atlas, the narrators are searching for Khôra, a place for being. Their travels are complex, their identities are multiple, but they all embark on a journey to express themselves and be free to collectively rewrite their stories. Along these lines, we want to mention the grassroots collective BAL ARCHITEKTEK and their initiative *Looking for Feminist Utopias.* Behind this project are architects Dominika Janicka, Barbara Nawrocka, and Dominika Wilczyńska from Poland. By asking a provocative question, 'What if we let women design for two years? Would they create a better world?' their aim is to investigate the fem-architects of the socialist era to give resonance to women's work in the field of architecture and promote feminist urban planning.

Readings that inspired us

Many books crossed our path while writing this Atlas. Some were new discoveries, and some were old-time loves. To mention only a few: *Invisible Cities* by Italo Calvino, *Common Space: The City as Commons* by Stavros Stavrides, the publications of *Writing Urban Places*, and of course, the journeys of Corto Maltese.

Image credits

All images by Sergios Strigklogiannis unless otherwise noted.

Notes

1 Roland Barthes, *Mythologies* (New York: The Noonday Press, 1972 [1991 print]), p.120.

2 A popular meme symbolising peoples' struggle and resistance against power, with its roots in a couplet by Dinos Christianopoulos:
καὶ τί δὲν κάνατε γιὰ νὰ μὲ
θάψετε ὅμως ξεχάσατε πὼς
ἤμουν σπόρος
[what didn't you do to bury me
but you forgot I was a seed.]
In *The Body and the Wormwood (1960–1993)*, translated into English by Prof. Nicholas Kostis (1995).

3 C.P. Cavafy, "Ithaka", in *C.P. Cavafy: Collected Poems*. Translated by Edmund Keeley and Philip Sherrard (New Jersey: Princeton University Press, 1975).

Atlas of Urban Mythologies
Francesca Cocchiara and Sergios Strigklogiannis

LINA Writing Award
a publishing project by dpr-barcelona
and the Irish Architecture Foundation

LINA
lina.community

LINA platform is coordinated by the Faculty
of Architecture of the University of Ljubljana

LINA team
Head of LINA Platform Matevž Čelik
Manager Mateja Kurir
Coordinator Nuša Zupanc
PR Coordinator Hana Cirman
Financial Coordinator Maja Bevc

Editorial coordinators César Reyes Nájera (dpr-barcelona)
and Blaithin Quinn (Irish Architecture Foundation)
Design Numa Merino Studio
Photos Sergios Strigklogiannis, studio inscape,
Vesna Petkovska, Saimir Kristo
Illustration Martin Fengel
Copy-editing and proofreading Daniel Lacasta Fitzsimmons
Editorial Assistance Clara Manigne-Malan

Printed in Spain
ISBN 978-84-124942-4-2
First published in May 2023

dpr-barcelona
Viladomat 59, 40 4a
08015 Barcelona
dpr-barcelona.com

Irish Architecture Foundation
15 Bachelors Walk
Dublin 1, Ireland. D01 EA02
architecturefoundation.ie

Irish Architecture Foundation

Co-funded by the European Union